A not G

By RL Lane

"What's that?" I asked him. "A painting I acquired", he said. It was standing up along a wall of his shop covered from view. He went on to say how someone offered him $400 for it, but he thought it was worth more so he didn't accept it. I asked him if I could see it…

He said he tried to figure out who the artist is, but he was unable to…

We uncovered it…

I looked at it. I could imagine the artist holding it up for the first time for his family to see. Brilliance shining from it. Even he was surprised at the outcome. The painting is just on a regular canvas as far as I can tell, but the art he constructed is anything but regular or ordinary. When light shines through the back of it, the sunset and water in the lake glisten. Completely brilliant. It was easy to see this was a masterpiece in the eyes of both the artist and the observer.

I had looked at the artist's signature in the lower right-hand corner. My computer screen just flashed. Rays of light angled across it. Oh. What is he trying to say? Is there something else in the lower right-hand corner of that picture? Perhaps hidden by the frame. Darryl said there is no artist by the name of G. Viani. I told him that is not a "G". You need to have a creative mind to see that the first letter was created…not just penned as an ordinary letter. The artist dragged the line of paint down at the end with the stroke of his brush.

Darryl went on to tell me how it was acquired, but he told me himself…

He flew in to Italy. Oh. The man. I just realized I have been talking to the man, not the artist. He flew into Italy…

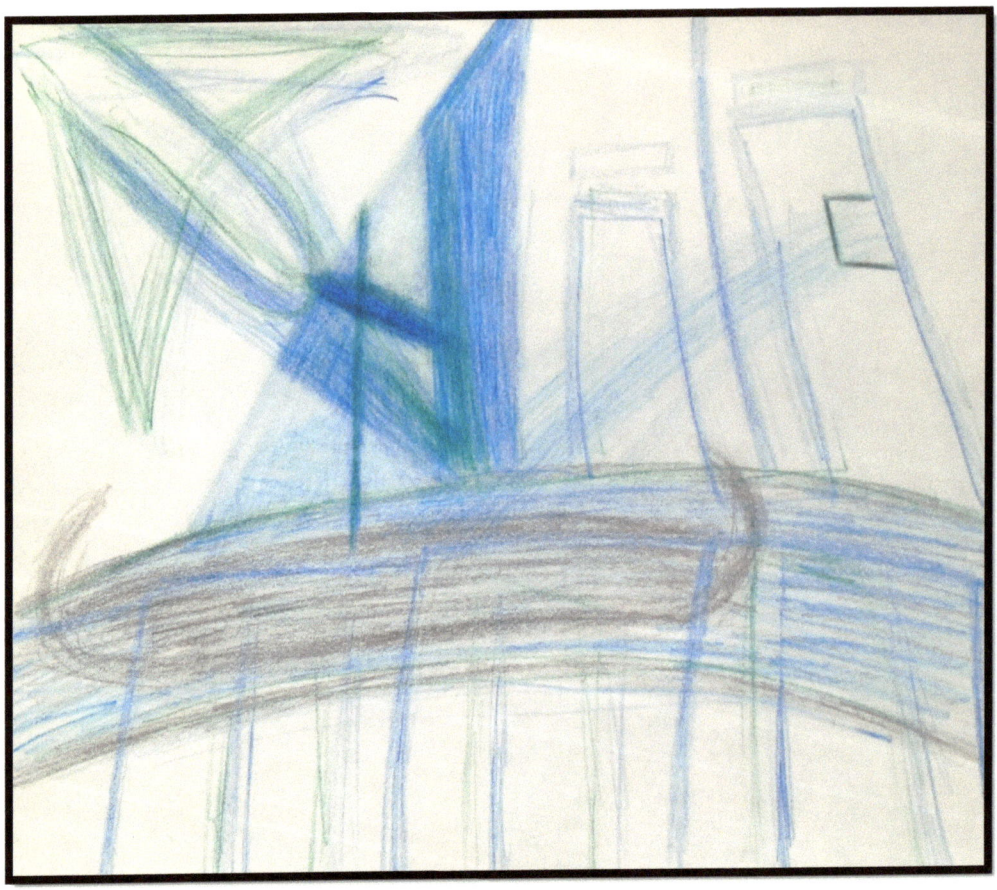

He had time before his return back to the states. He was a pilot. A US pilot.
He was walking through the streets of the little Italian village. There was
something about the street sign near where Alberto Viani's shop was. Perhaps he
recognized the street sign. Perhaps it was the same town where Alberto Viani lived.
The painting was hanging on a wall of the shop just waiting to be looked upon. To
be admired. Alberto Viani himself was there that day. He was excited the pilot
would take home his work and it would travel to the United States. He had respect
for the pilot who would hang it in his home.

The painting would remind the pilot of his own Italian heritage. It would
remind him of his travels around the world. It was acquired in the 1950s. It hung
in his home all his life. It did not transfer hands…

The painting was special to Alberto. He constructed it at the mid-point of
his life. Oh. That is funny. My screen just flashed and rays of light angled across
it again. Oh. He did not construct it at the mid-point of his life? The painting is so
special because of how he used the light. It is a mystery to me whenever I look at
it. I don't actually want to know how he created it. I just want to be able to help
prove it is his work…

The cover of your book is how he designed his first initial. The letter A. The bolded part within the capital A is what is on the painting. I am not sure what the letter is next to it. Perhaps that is how he initially contemplated drawing it. You can see how the final letter could be mistaken for a G…

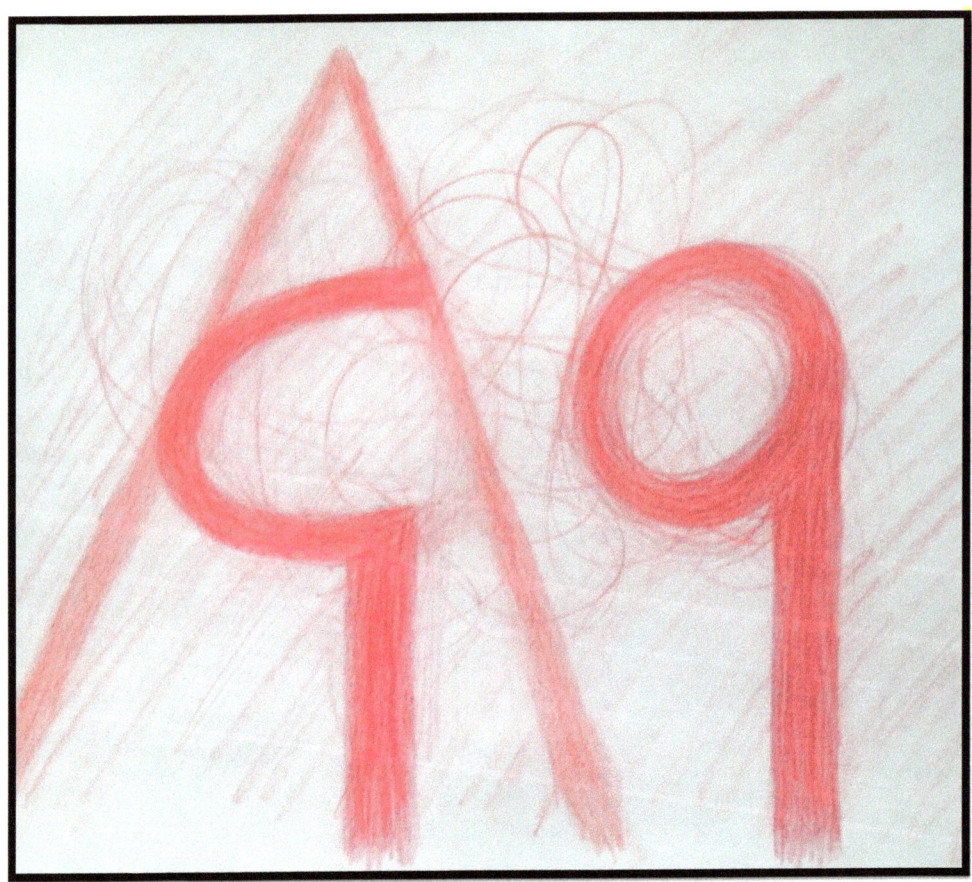

We know that Alberto signed his name A. Viani, but if this painting is the only one where he used that signature, the auction houses will not be able to prove it is his work. There is someone out there in the Viani family who knows what this painting meant to the great Alberto.

Alberto was more known for his sculptures. That is partly why this painting is so special. There were far fewer paintings done by this talented man.

The place that is shown in his painting…

a lake, the mountains,

Northern Italy,

a small cabin in the woods,

the sky.

The brilliance.

The artist was born in 1906 and died in 1989. He says he made the painting in 19... He hasn't told me yet when he made it. I hope he does before we get to the end of this book.

I still feel like there is something else in this painting. Something hidden that would identify it as Alberto's work. Oh. Are we supposed to hold it up to the light at an angle? Is that why the rays of light flashed across my screen at an angle...

Sometimes artists recreate another artist's work. Here is the RL Lane version of Alberto's painting…

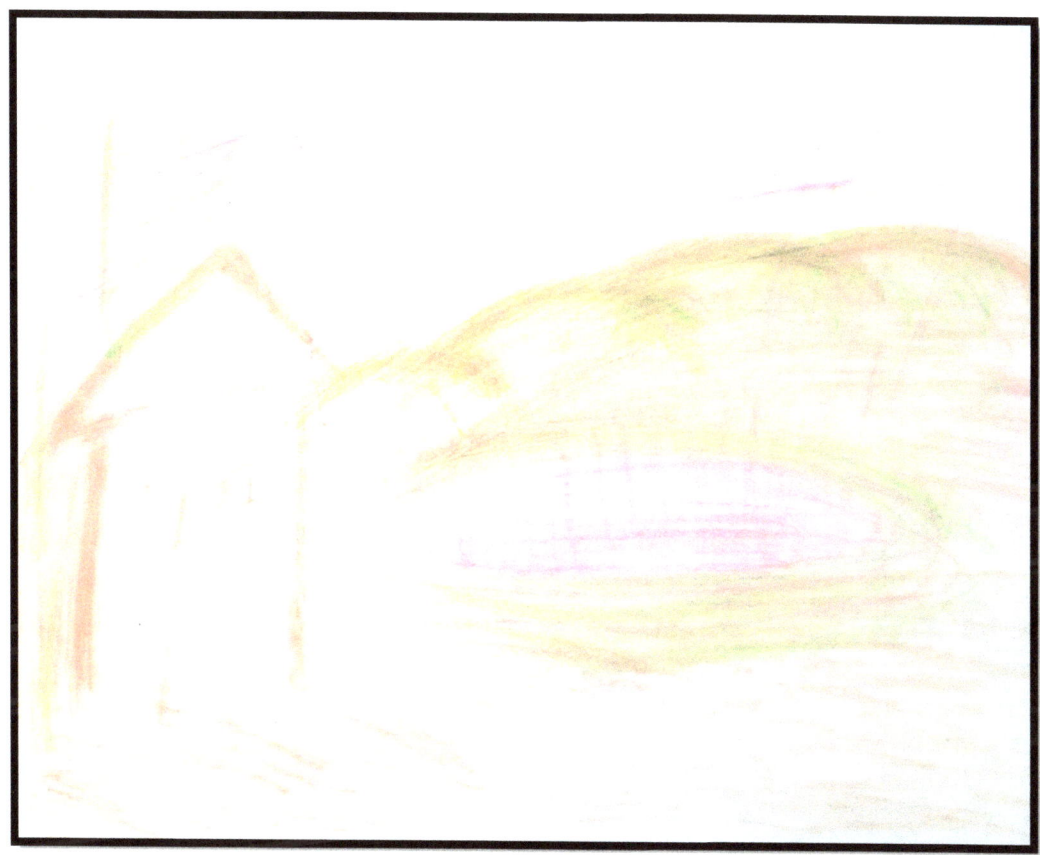

I don't think Alberto wants his work recreated or reproduced. It was the only one. It was always meant to be just one.

You can tell that time has altered it from its original fresh coat of paint. I look at it and can imagine Alberto sitting on his stool, laboring over his picture. I wonder if he ever doubted what the final product would become. Someone just commented to me today that I have no doubt about my own work. They said that a lot of artist's do. It is different for me perhaps because I never know what I am creating. I just do it. Perhaps if I knew, I would worry about where to add this line or that color…

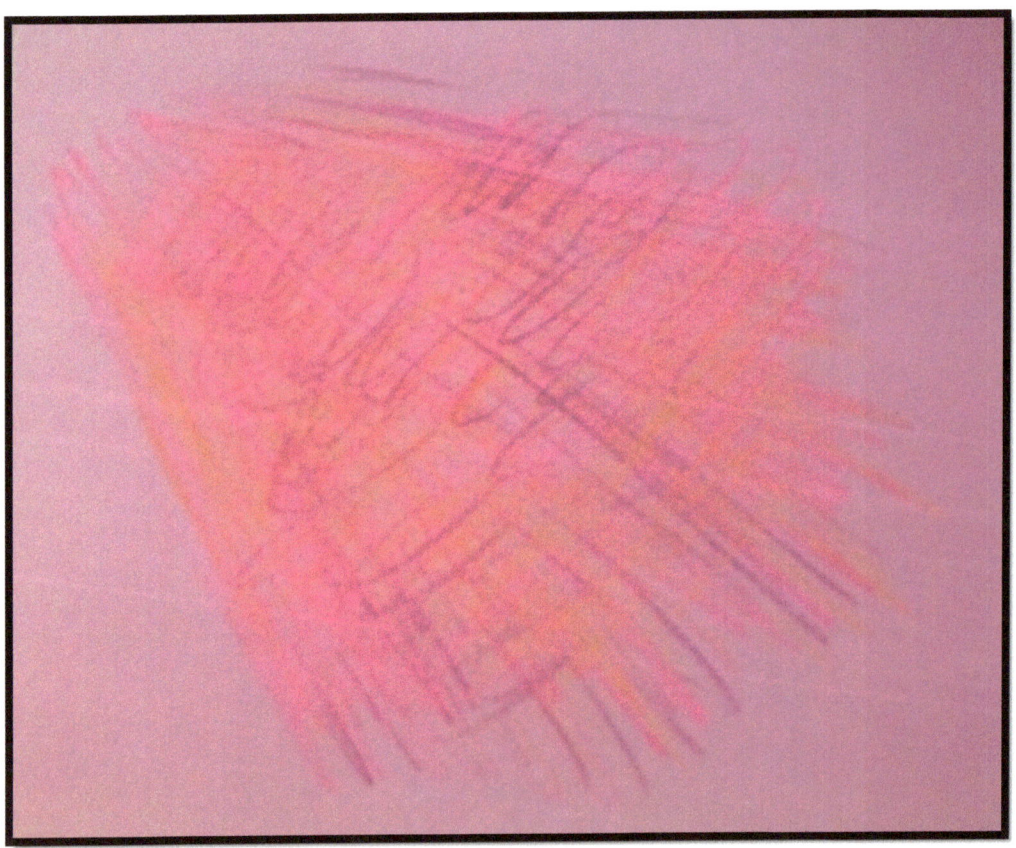

Dear Italy,

We have your painting. It is here in the United States. Can you please get this story to the Viani family. I can be reached at RosaLeeeLane@gmail.com.

We really do need the Viani family's help. I am counting on the UK readers to let your friends in Italy know about this book and the painting. I do not actually have any readers from Italy yet.

It is not about money. It is about honoring this extremely talented man and his unique work. Anyone who knew him I'm sure would agree he would not want his special painting floating around the states in the hands of someone who didn't even know it was his work of art.

The dot at the end… He purposely placed a dot at the end of his name. He is…was

Alberto Viani.

"The letters of their name would scroll across the television screen. The "y" on the end was drawn with a loop in it which made it look like a "p", so for years I wondered who Disnep was..." RL Lane

I am not sure why that paragraph about Disney is still there. It is already in "The Vault". I thought I had deleted all the pages when I used it as a template for this book.

"1938", they keep on saying. It makes me wonder if the 1938 goes to the year the painting was created or to something Mr. Disney created that is in "The Vault" that I have re-drawn. Oh Wait! Is Walt saying something in this book is also his?!

The Empty Chair

I hope the Viani family doesn't mind I added this section to their book. It is about the empty chair. It is important. I was inside but could easily see it sitting there. It looked so alone. It was outside on the deck. The breeze was blowing slightly, but the chair was sitting so still. No one was in it. Can the readers please look at all the empty chairs and sit in one of them now. If it is a Sunday, go look right now. Find the nearest one. Pull it out, and take a seat. Tell the spirits to move aside while you have a rest. They already got to live their lives. It's your turn now to fill the seat.

It is a Presidential election year next year in the Unites States. A woman will try again to take the seat. Is it our turn now? I wondered if Italy has ever had a female President. I looked online…

Italy has lagged far behind its European Union counterparts in achieving equality for women. Women are still expected to be the main caregivers in the family. The employment rate for women was only about forty-six percent in 2012. In the south, only thirty percent of women are employed. Six percent of the board members of Italy's largest listed companies are women, compared to twenty-two percent in France.

Dear Italy Women,

Are you sad to just be Moms? Are you sad to not have to work and take care of a family plus help make the decisions plus…

Or are you, the happiest women in Europe?

Oh. 1938. That year. I googled it and Italy. It was still the Kingdom of Italy.

The Italian Racial Laws were in effect from 1938 to 1943 to enforce racial discrimination. These were directed against the Italian Jews and the native inhabitants of the colonies.

Oh. This is what we were supposed to find...

The Walt Disney Company's Italian division. It is headquartered in the beautiful city of Milan. The company was founded on 8 May 1938. The company owns and operates Disney Channel Italy, Disney in English, plus they also publish comics.

Oh. I am working on the first RL Lane comic. I wonder if I can send them a proof of it. I wonder if they will help RL Lane to get it published...

Walt's company is too big for an independent artist to get to them. Somehow I found IDW Digital Comics. I found a contact email. I could send them a draft of McUmbria. Will they be the ones to help RL Lane get these characters to the comics...

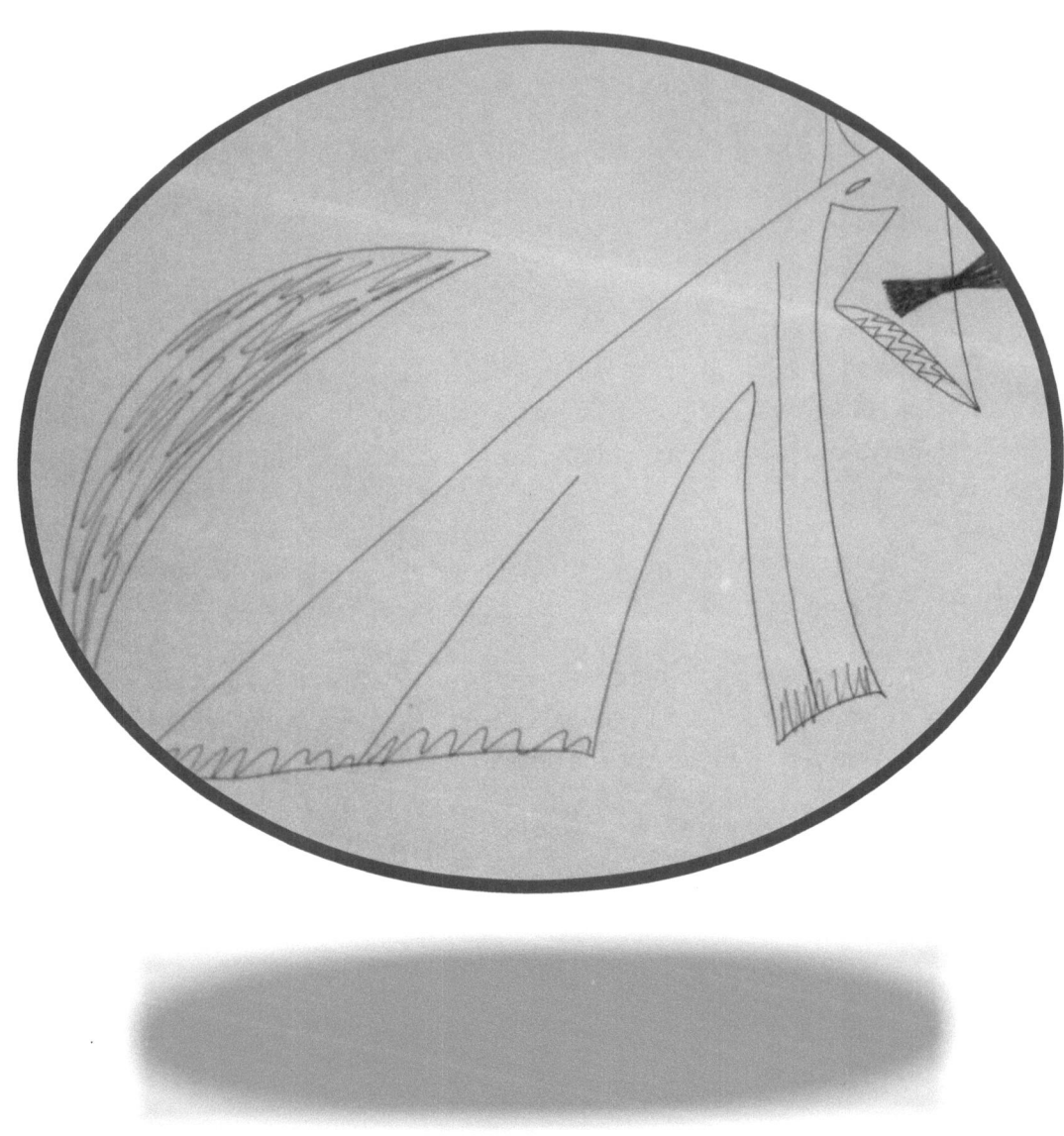

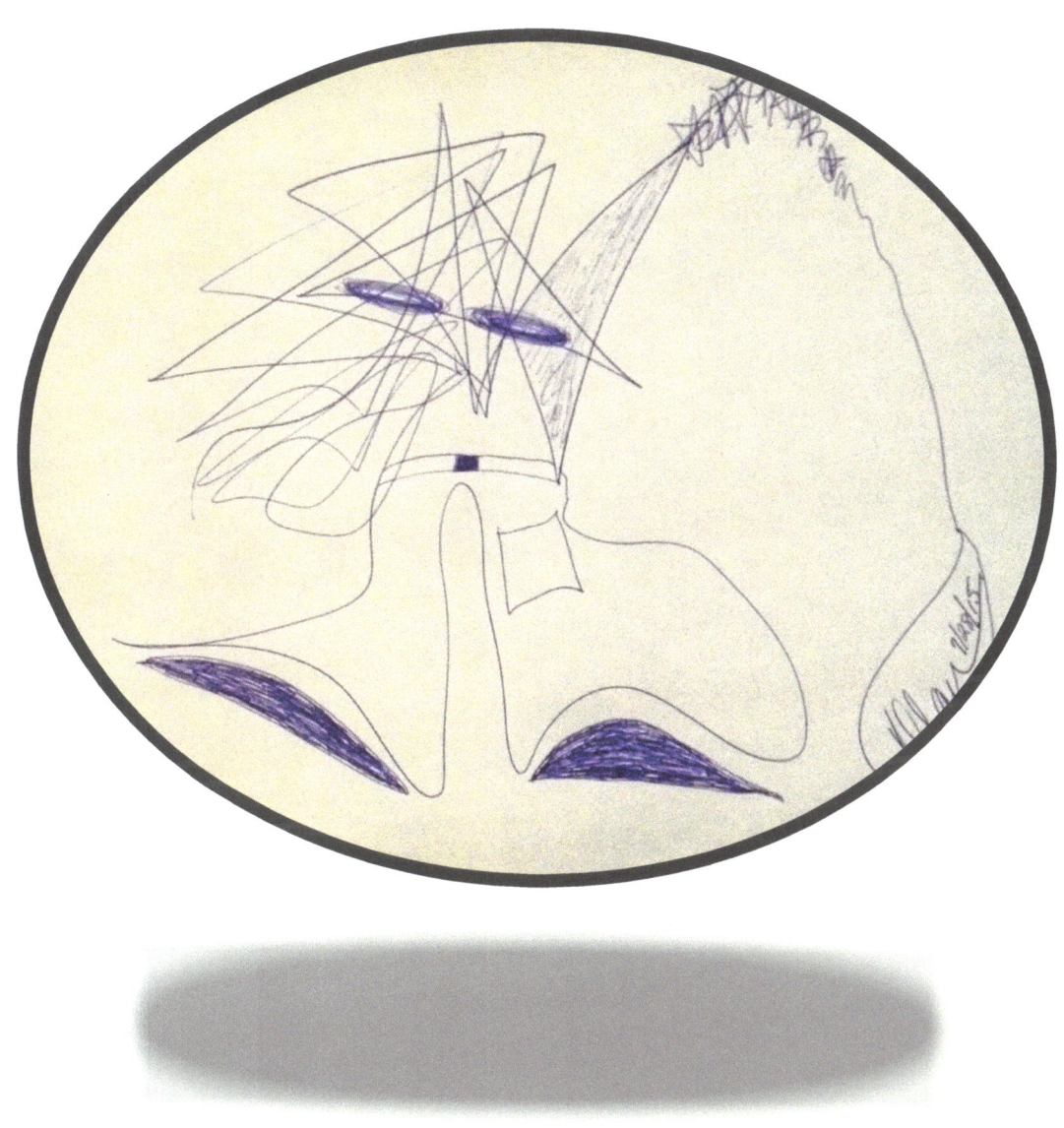

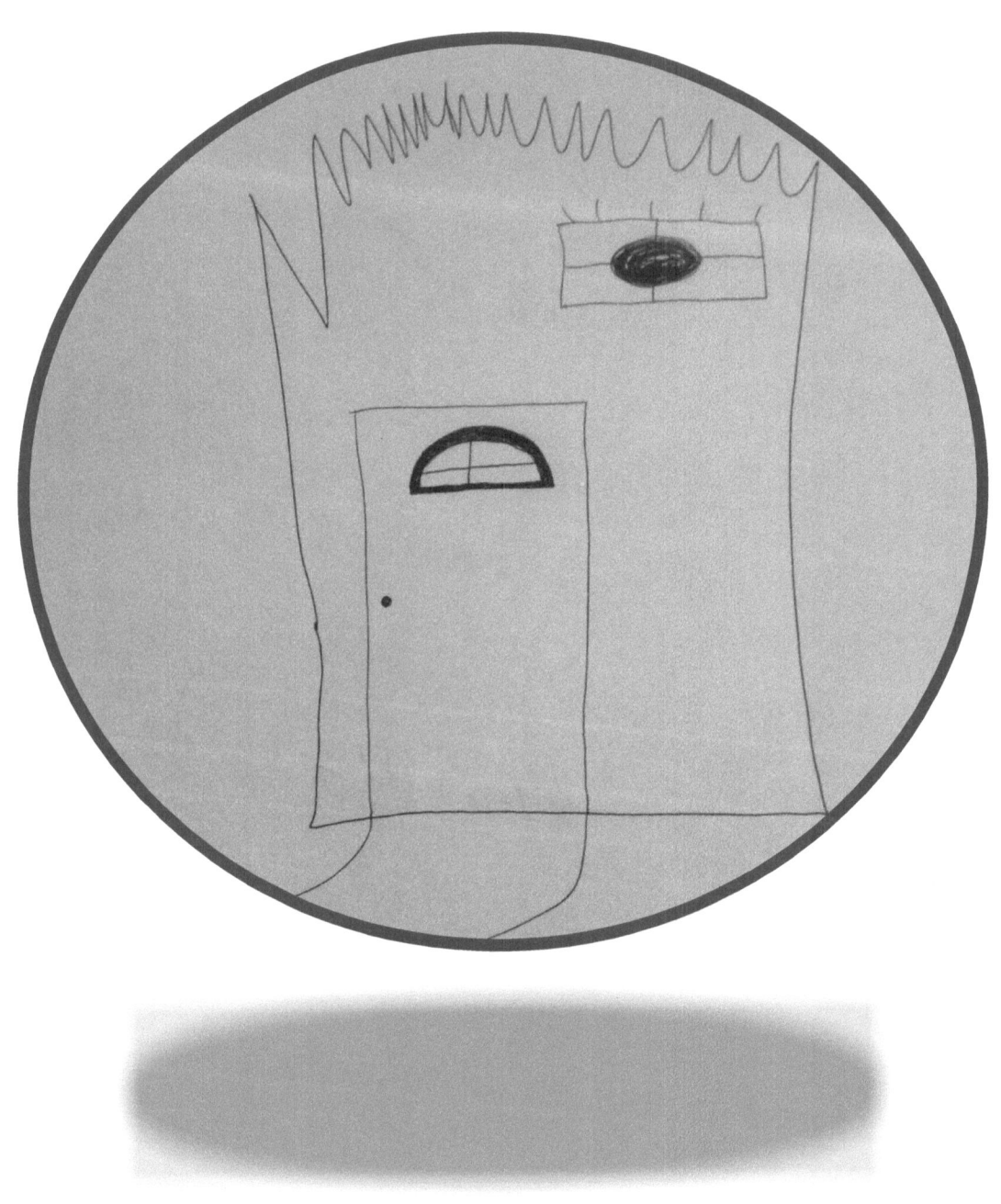

"McUmbria"

About the Author and *Illustrator*

RL Lane has published the EcarreT series and a collection of short story art books featuring the author's illustrations. The EcarreT series begins with "Chapel Street Signs"…

…unexplained connections that challenge us to beli ve. A woman, a Dad a Doctor, a cat and mouse, a horse and tale tell their stories. "Do you beli ve in spirits?" I asked my friend. "Well look", he said, "I believe there are things that cannot be explained…" Oh. Plus, hear ov a Mom's battle with her struggle to connect to the woman…her little girl.

Welcome to EcarreT…a world
Where everyone cares
Why did I have to create it in…

A fiction fantasy world?

You may already know why, but you will see regardless of what you believe as a girl's journey of love and faith on her "Touring Machine" take her on the best journey of her mundane life. A life well on its way takes a turn in a direction that could've never been seen or even dreamed…

The author can be contacted at:

RosaLeeeLane@gmail.com
www.Amazon.com/author/readrllane

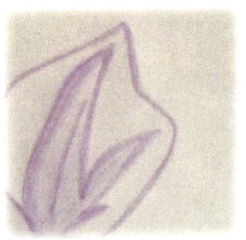

www.ingramcontent.com/pod-product-compliance
Lightning Source LLC
Chambersburg PA
CBHW050432180526
45159CB00006B/2509